OAK:

Business Principles of Strategic and Operational Excellence

Vincent Kwapong

Copyright © 2015 Vincent Kwapong
Book-broker Publishers of Florida
Port Charlotte, FL 33980
Printed in the United States of America
ISBN 978-0-9963076-5-9

<u>Contents</u>

Introduction

How do I grow margins on my staple products and services while continuing to innovate to grow top line? What are the key prerequisites to establishing a sustaining culture of operations excellence and operations innovations?

Answers to these questions are not self-evident nor are they alike when you compare highly successful companies to those lagging behind.

For business leaders and shareholders the ultimate desire is an organizational culture that takes to heart the essence of continuous improvement as a prerequisite for excellence.

Whether your scope of responsibility is at the department level, division level or the business franchise unit, operations excellence and operations innovation need to become a characteristic of your organization in order to maximize the delivery of value to customers. This book is about making that happen.

Trained as systems engineer with background in electrical, materials science and industrial engineering principles as well as finance, I have always been interested in understanding the drivers of business performance across different industries.

Over my 25 years of work experience I have had the privilege of working with diverse companies from Johnson and Johnson to General Electric, Sony Electronics to British Telecom, SC Johnson to Goldman Sachs, from United Technologies to Asahi Glass.

This experience has given me insight into key drivers of success for companies. This insight is what I am sharing as the OAK business principles of strategic and operational excellence.

While the information being shared in this book is not new, I have attempted to aggregate and highlight the key elements that matter most.

This book summarizes experiences and knowledge I have acquired from all my mentors at these companies that gave me guidance, the lessons learned, as well as the success celebrated.

1: What Do You Want?

Two traditional bibles of business ethics and practices are Adam Smith's *Wealth of Nations* and Napoleon Hill's *Think and Grow Rich*. Both books take a tangential approach to business success. One, *Wealth of Nations*, focuses on the indirect benefits of a successful business or individual to the community. Smith describes this process of community enrichment as the invisible hand syndrome: as a man or business grows, an increasing pool of people benefits from that success. For example, if a man lives well enough to afford an accountant and personal assistant, his success means two people now have jobs.

Likewise, when a business does well, that means both more jobs for employees and more products to benefit an expanding base of satisfied customers.

Hill's book explains financial success in terms of the Golden Rule: Do unto others as you would have them do unto you. Hill was right; think of how you'd feel if someone didn't deliver to you what she promised. Besides, if members of your management and manufacturing teams practiced that age-old rule, productivity would pop.

But Hill doesn't suggest that women and men who control large quantities of resources and people should just strive to be nice. That's not why you're running a business—it certainly isn't how you'll stay in business!

Instead, he argues that planning and visioning how to make money is the first step to success; treating people with dignity and respect is a major investment in your drive to material success.

Or, as Eliyahu M. Goldratt writes in *The Goal*, you're in business to make money. Yes, you create connections and inventions, conveniences and lifesavers, fads and ideas, or services and supplies. But all those products have to be brought together, assembled, and distributed, be they intellectual property or steel beams.

As you grow your business you make jobs and friends. But those are collateral benefits, daily examples of Adam Smith's Invisible Hand theory. Others benefit as you do well. But that's not why you do business, you do it to make money.

2: The Oak Tree

As Napoleon Hill explains, first you need a plan. And that plan must work as an organism, each part contributing to the benefit of the whole. The mighty oak, whose name is an acronym for the process you'll learn about in this book, exemplifies such a creation. The taproot finds moisture, the trunk protects and lifts the tree, the branches expands it reach, and the leaves convert sunlight to food. The parts work in harmony. Besides, a healthy tree is green, like money!

The different parts working together create something solid and strong. Just as successful businesses build for the future, for durability, oaks take about 20 years to reach maturity. A healthy oak tree in essence, is like a community much in the same way as an organization is.

Key elements of the community are the PEOPLE, ASSETS, and REPUTATION: These elements have to be managed and nurtured to deliver and perform to clearly defined expectations. While the basic building blocks do not change, the core functional role of the organization whether it is producing widgets (as in manufacturing) or delivering intangible set of value-added activities (such as service business) dictates the approach to use. Here I would stress the importance of the human factor, both the external culture of the workplace and society (people have different expectations today, for example few people expect to stay at the same job all their lives; workplaces are more diverse, there are fewer gender-specific jobs and minorities or others who once were invisible now have roles that have attained near-equality. These are all modern factors that impact the human resources.

OAK is based on a continuous improvement methodology that focuses on improving both quality and productivity. The OAK principles of continuous improvement maximizes the flow of value to customers and investors by putting customer needs and expectations first.

Value added to the human component and the operating environment should translate

into value added to the finished product, thus making it more attractive and more able to command market share or consumer preference

These needs and expectations include wanting a business that provides high quality products and services, on-time delivery, responsiveness, and a rewarding value-enhancing relationship.

The OAK concept requires three elements to be in place:

- **O**wnership - as in whose neck is on the line and understands that her success and that of the organization are linked.
- **A**ccountability - who has the leadership role and will be acknowledging and assuming responsibility for all related actions and attainment of success within the scope of a role (or defined responsibility)? Included in this accountability will be establishment of clear metrics of success.
- **K**nowledge - to get the job done means, among other things, that individuals who have the Ownership and Accountability for a specific initiative also have the deep functional, technical, or role expertise to get the job done. It also means making provisions through training and other skills development activities to equip members of the organization with the

knowledge and tools to carry out their responsibilities.

These three elements are critical prerequisites that must be established in order to stand a chance of achieving success at operations excellence. There are no by-standers in this vision. It costs money to maintain idle resources that are not producing.

A tree wants to grow; a business wants to make money. All customers are looking for financial results. Successful leadership and the use of the OAK operating principles by all employees, allow a business to balance and meet all its stakeholders' expectations.

3: Road Trip

Once when you got behind the wheel for a long drive, you made sure you had a map, or that the route had been planned. These days, a Garmin or other GPS device can do that job. But still, you would seldom go somewhere without finding out how to get there. So why should you take your business on a road trip without mapping the route?

When we talk about achieving excellence the point is really to be successful with your customers and make them as profitable as possible. You can't stand still. You have to figure out continuously what is it that means most to your customers and strive to improve and drive customer growth and revenue maximization.

Now, how do you do it? This is when a strategic roadmap becomes necessary. It determines where we

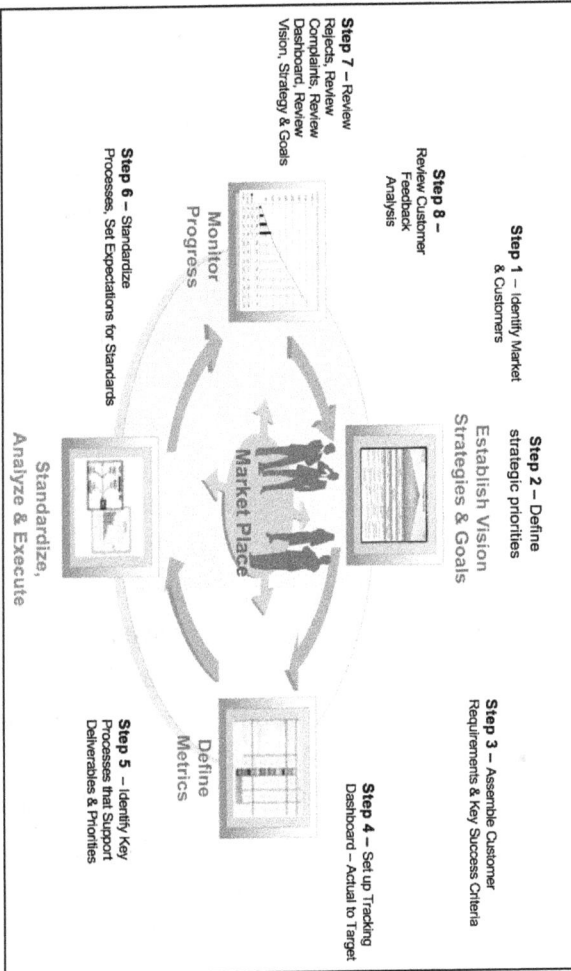

Figure 1: Operations Excellence Process Flow

Step 1 – Identify Market & Customers

Step 2 – Define strategic priorities

Establish Vision Strategies & Goals

Step 3 – Assemble Customer Requirements & Key Success Criteria

Step 4 – Set up Tracking Dashboard – Actual to Target

Define Metrics

Step 5 – Identify Key Processes that Support Deliverables & Priorities

Step 6 – Standardize Processes, Set Expectations for Standards

Standardize, Analyze & Execute

Step 7 – Review Rejects, Review Complaints, Review Dashboard, Review Vision, Strategy & Goals

Monitor Progress

Step 8 – Review Customer Feedback Analysis

Market Place

start from and where we want to end up in order to achieve the initial objectives I spelled out. The strategy roadmap, updated annually, includes the highest level objectives for the business. Once the strategy is set, each subgroup in the organization can use this document as an input to create its own set of goals and initiatives. This overlapping and cascading approach to strategy deployment ensures alignment to the overall goals and objectives. From this point, individual objectives for each person in the organization can be created.

The subgroups' plan represents tactics which ensure the success of the overall strategy.

Before you can embark on the journey of operations excellence you need to have an overall strategy, a business plan of how you're going to achieve the key performance objectives that you set for yourself.

That strategy must have specific, achievable, clear goals that the entire business can strive to achieve. What are the key elements that we're going to choose to do to help us successfully achieve those goals and what are those pieces that we're choosing not to go after because they represent distractions?

Operations Strategy

Years ago I worked with a large multi-billion dollar pharmaceutical company. I was in new product development, which entailed defining manufacturing requirements for new products. I had several years of manufacturing experience under my belt but was sort of rusty, as I had just returned to work after taking time off to earn my MBA.

The company had just discovered a new drug that improved the efficacy of stents. Stents traditionally used mechanical applications to force open clogged arteries to alleviate strokes.

However, one of nature's defense mechanisms is to attack any foreign item that enters the body. So the mechanical stents were soon covered by scar tissue. Ironically, although the stents were designed to mechanically open and clear clogged arteries, their very presence created the same problem because of the scar tissue.

To mitigate this we coated the stents with drugs that inhibited the growth of scar tissue. We had to get the improved system to market quickly before any other company could compete; two other companies had applications for approval pending with the FDA.

Unfortunately, in the race to get it to the market we expedited the manufacturing process without planning for the downstream mechanisms of getting products to the end user, the patient.

Additionally, once the FDA approval was received and a date set for market launch, not much emphasis was placed on how we were going to match demand to product availability. That led to two problems:

First, the ramp-up for the new system marked the first time the pharmaceutical and medical device communities sought joint approval of a product. Prior to that, the discrete industries had been regulated by two distinct branches of the FDA.

The pharmaceutical element required strict temperature control through the downstream supply chain of the product, from manufacture to installation, for it to maintain its pharmacological properties. There was no clear strategy for how this was going to be done at a reasonable cost. The result was that some products were stored in warehouses that did not have climate control or on unrefrigerated delivery trucks where they were exposed to temperature extremes that degraded their efficacy.

The company had to cut production to the point where it could only provide just-in-time point-to-point air delivery to doctors who were ready to install the devices. FDA standards forced us to go back to the drawing board and spend millions of dollars developing a comprehensive strategy and roadmap for delivering the product to its customers.

The loss of time and momentum gave our competitors the time they needed to get their FDA approvals and enter the market. They learned from our mistakes. The net impact was a significant loss of market share that ran into the hundreds of million dollars.

The second issue was related to initial customer demand. The company failed to develop that initial robust operations strategy for how they were going to meet that demand for the product. Leading up to the FDA approval, the marketing demand did a wonderful job of marketing the significant benefits of the product and shared with customers the target date for availability.

But we did such a good job building demand that we were not ready to meet orders. So when the launch date came around a whole host of customers that had placed orders could not get the product because of the time it took to manufacture and supply it. The company failed to put in place the initial shelf stock required to support day one's product launch. We lost valuable customer trust in our ability to deliver.

Lesson Learned

Today, companies like Apple and Samsung, as they get ready to launch new products, go to great lengths to plan operations strategies that integrate marketing requirements with supply chain requirements. Strategy is about making the choices and plans that you believe will get you where you and your business need to go. The operational activities and the tactics you employ become the core of your operations strategy. Once you have that starting point, then we must develop the road map to support that strategy.

A clear vision and the strategy to achieve that vision is thus an essential starting point for any effort to improve performance. The strategy defines direction and aligns the efforts of every individual in the organization toward a common destination and purpose. It identifies specific goals for how the business will serve its customers, employees, and shareholders.

Here we have both the Golden Rule and the OAK principles working in harmony. Neither the consistent members of your manufacturing team nor the consuming public want surprises. In making sure that you plan for demand and delivery as part of the product development process, you maximize the chances for success while minimizing the risk of frustrating employees or alienating customers.

The key here is the OAK principles of Ownership, Accountability, and Knowledge.

Ownership entails the members of the team being thoroughly versed as to their role in the grand vision. Accountability entails designating team members who will be responsible for realizing their portion of the road trip or vision. And knowledge is essential as all members of the team must be made aware of the regulatory, cultural, mechanical, and ancillary parameters of the mission.

The Metrics of Accountability

Your strategy document should integrate a set of goals that are important for meeting the needs of customers. Those goals should be balanced and represent all the stakeholder interests of the group including customer value and satisfaction, leadership, culture and environment, product, process and service excellence, and business results. Figure 2: *Sample OAK Dashboard* shows how one might establish specific metrics, with goals and measuring frequency tied into key strategic areas.

Goals are ideally expressed in terms of numeric values so that desired outcomes are clear and measurable over a 12-month period. Supporting the goals are a variety of specific initiatives and actions to be pursued to achieve the stated goals.

Main View SERVICE COMPANY XYZ		Jul-13
Plant/Function Performance	**Owner**	**Year-End Goal**
Region or Functional Area	EAST		
	NORTH		
	WEST		
	SOUTH		

Strategic Alignment	Metrics	Owner	Year-End Goal
Process	Productivity		
Revenue Growth	Revenue Per Tech ($)		
Margin Expansion	Unproductive Time (%)		
Revenue Growth	Revenue per Customer ($)		
Margin Expansion	Overtime - Nonbillable (%)		
Process	Install Projects		
Revenue Growth	Backlog Sales		
Margin Expansion	Backlog Margin		
Margin Expansion	Executed Margin		
Revenue Growth	% Quote Closed		
Revenue Growth	Rev per Install Tech		
Process	Service		
Margin Expansion	Conversion Rate (%)		
Revenue Growth	On-time Completion (%)		
Revenue Growth	Service Call-backs (%)		
Margin Expansion	Service Mix (%)		
Revenue Growth	Service Contract (% New)		
Process	Billing / AR		
Revenue Growth	CIP Coverage (%)		
Revenue Growth	DSO (Days)		

Figure 2: Sample OAK Dashboard

Current-Month Goal	**Jan**	**Feb**	**Mar**	**Q1 Average**

Current-Month Goal	**Jan**	**Feb**	**Mar**	**Q1 Average**

You can't improve something if you can't measure so essentially being able to measure performance is going to be absolutely critical. So we'll talk about essentially defining what those key metrics are and how you measure them to be able to drive improvement

Now I stress that part for a reason: you don't want to measure for the sake of measuring. That's not going to get you anywhere. That speaks to The Uncertainty Principle, a theory that says there is no way that you can accurately know the position of anything and measure it without influencing it.

Whatever it is you're going to measure make sure it's for the right reason, at the right time, because otherwise you're influencing it in the wrong direction.

Assign Ownership and Metrics

To be most effective in encouraging the right behavior and guiding performance goals should be assigned to specific individuals with clear expectations of what success means.

Directly linking personal performance objectives to the overall goals of the organization is a powerful way to motivate individual and maximize team results

Customer	Employees	Sales/Rev	Service	Installation
AR Metrics (aging, top 10 invoices, etc)	Turnover	Orders	On-time inspection	Timely completion
Top 5 customers	# of HC vs Plan	WIP ($)	Revenue by Monitoring, D&C, T&I (and related margins)	Revenue (and related margins)
Customer satisfaction survey (NPS)	Satisfaction survey	Sales Person (versus quota)	Overtime (chargeable vs non-chargeable)	Overtime (chargeable vs non-chargeable)
Growth/Erosion (by customer)	Revenue / employee	Pipeline (Quotes outstanding). What's out there but not quoted.	Contract metrics (# new contracts, # renewable, # lost)	WIP scheduling (inventory of jobs and status)
Customer mix (% end user, etc)	HC by area or fns,	Quotes by segment	Downtime (non-billable)	Downtime (non-billable)
			Conversions (warranty, pull-thru)	

Figure 3: Establish Metrics for Key Business Areas

Dashboard & Leading Indicators Benefits

- Proactive vs reactive

- Early detection of out of control limit indicators

- Positive cultural change
  - *Aligns the Organization on goals*
  - *Ask the Right Questions*
  - *Enabler to Manage Facts*
  - *Holistic tool for communication and decision making*

The Goal of a Dashboard is not to measure, but to improve the Business.

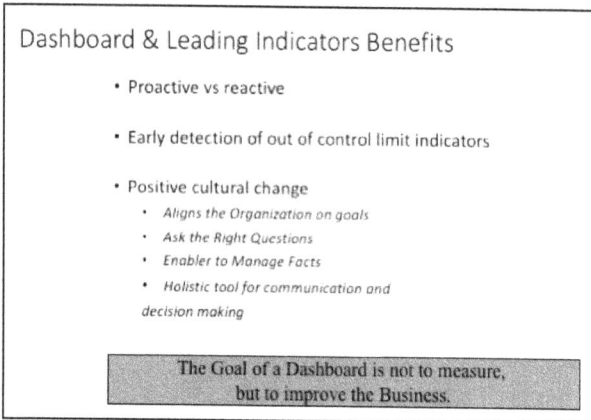

Figure 4: Dashboard metrics should lead and not lag

The Strategic Dashboard

On the operational strategy piece there are five key elements. Once you know where you want your business to go, that's your destination. The strategic dashboard has to take each of these elements and make sure that it organizes, defines, and guides the business to the target. The dashboard is the collection of the key measures for each of your strategic elements to help you understand whether you are moving forward, at a standstill, or not making progress.

It's how you take your business's temperature in the short run, for the long haul it's what you use to measure your progress toward your goal. Figure 3: *Establish Metrics for Key Business Areas* illustrates

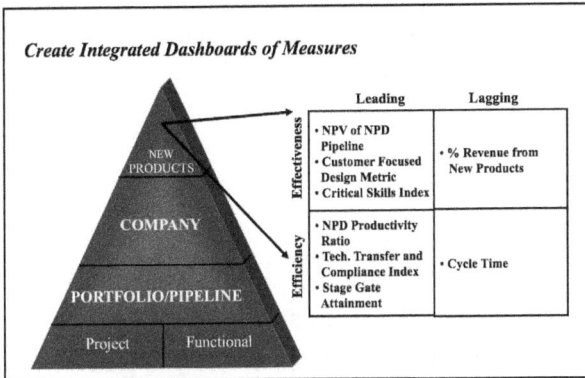

Figure 5: Establish leading metrics for your dashboard

examples of metrics that can be defined to measure different business value streams. Thinking through and making sure there are direct linkages between the business bottom line and key leading activities that are measurable can pay big dividend.

In a previous role with a big multinational, I had a product that a lot of our customers were raving about. Yet, revenue for that product line was not seeing any growth. We pulled a team together and laid out the "transfer function" for generating revenue. The transfer function establishes the cause and effect relationship between different activities and their net output.

For the mathematically inclined it may be simplified as:

$Y = f(x_1, x_2, x_3, \ldots x_n)$ where the x's serve as leading indicators. Through further analysis we came to implement specific changes on how we contacted customers that netted an additional $600MM in revenue (see Figure 5: *Establish Leading Metrics for Your Dashboard*).

Value Proposition

Once you can articulate the value proposition products that you sell or the service you provide you have defined those elements that need to be preserved. In the course of selling or providing that service you need to make sure that your employees understand what is important for you to provide to your customers. This is also where you identify what customers you're supplying and what value that customer is deriving from your product or service.

Product Description and Value Proposition

The second item is the description of your value proposition. If you're making widgets, what is it about that product that makes it valuable to your customers? You need to articulate the products or the proposed products that you're trying to sell and what it is about them makes them attractive.

Likewise, if you're in the service business you must analyze the nature of that service and the value that your customers derive from it.

What if your widget offers functionality at the lowest cost? A similar product may be available from other vendors or suppliers but no one can match your cost.

Or what if customers could only get your widget from you? For example, you can only buy and sells iPhone from Apple. Although Apple is essentially just selling a commodity—a phone—the software that runs on it is proprietary product of Apple. If you want an iPhone, you have to pay Apple or forget it.

In contrast, if you want a phone that uses the Android system, you can buy one from Samsung, HP, Lenova, or other android phone device manufacturers.

Besides, those phones are cheaper. So if a customer's idea of value is lowest possible cost, that's where they'll most likely get their smart phone.

Those examples illustrate how when you know your product—what it can do, why it can do it, and if customers want it—that makes it possible to craft an accurate value proposition.

That speaks to the Knowledge component of the OAK method, understanding the environment and culture in which you hope your business will survive—and thrive.

Key Marketing and Regulatory Requirements

When in Rome, as they say, we do as the Romans do. Like most clichés, that one lives on because it has a strong element of truth. Most products have to conform to some regulatory requirements, which is often unique to the region in which you plan to do business.

If you're going to introduce a product or service in a particular part of the world, your corporate knowledge base must include up-to-date information about that region's regulatory requirements.

If it doesn't, you could be asking for trouble. Consider Uber, the popular ride-sharing program. Uber provides a platform that allow customers looking for rides to link up with individuals who have cars in the area and can provide those rides. Uber is doing well in a lot of places with their product, which is a cheap alternative to traditional taxi and limousine services.

Now in some locations you don't need any license to essentially provide that kind of service. But you do need licensing in New York City. As populous as it is New York City would seem a natural environment for a ride-sharing platform. But the city has very strict regulations in terms of who can provide rides to customers the drivers don't know.

Uber ran into a brick wall maintained with vigor by the whole New York City taxi industry. But that experience was a drive in the park compared to what happened when Uber went to Germany. There, Uber wound up facing significant fines.

If Uber executives had done their homework, they could have avoided a lot of headache. The business is a ride-sharing platform, not a social engineering or litigating entity. The regulatory skirmishes consumed energy and resources Uber could have invested elsewhere or accumulated as profit. That's an expensive lesson.

And if you remember my earlier story about the medical device I helped produce, if you're looking to sell something that has some claim of health improvement or disease amelioration, you can't just go out and sell it and make those claims. You need to get regulatory approval for those things.

But sometimes ignorance of culture, the zeitgeist of the region in which you plan to do business, is equally fatal.

Doug Lansky, a writer for The Huffington Post, sums this up in epic form in a column posted July 20, 2010 titled *The Funniest Marketing Fails of All Time*. In part, he wrote:

You may have heard about some of the classic cases where marketing went wrong. Remember Pepsi's slogan "Come Alive with the Pepsi Generation"? In Taiwan, that translated as "Pepsi brings your ancestors back from the dead." KFC's "Finger Lickin' Good" translated in Chinese as "Eat your fingers off." And then there was Sweden's famous vacuum-cleaner promo: "Nothing Sucks like Electrolux."

[http://www.huffingtonpost.com/doug-lansky/the-funniest-marketing-fa_b_652426.html]

For years, the granddaddy of cultural fails was the story of Chevrolet's efforts to sell a car called the Nova, which reportedly meant "no go" in Spanish. The story is a myth, but its persistence speaks to the importance of gathering accurate knowledge of the environment and landscape in which you will be doing business.

Operations Objectives and Scope

Let's return for a moment to the oak tree metaphor I used earlier. Strong roots are analogous to firm, factual knowledge such as company lore and market evaluations. Limbs are like branches, spreading the brand and product as far as the support systems can reach. And leaves are like a marketing department, attracting contacts and converting them to customers.

That's a description of a heathy tree—or a healthy business climate where ownership, accountability, and knowledge are synthesized and synchronized for a specific goal.

But you can't take for granted that everyone in the operations is doing what they need to do to support your company's vision. So here's the other piece that needs to be clearly articulated

The issue could be as specific as tracking how many products do we need to sell in a month to maintain your vision. Who's accountable for making those sales? Does she share and understand the vision? What's in it for her and her department?

Our operations need to be set up so that the cost of making that product gives us a profit, of course, but that's not all. What about the quality of what you make? What about the capacity to get it to market, or the efficiency of the supply lines? Who's minding those stores? And in what knowledge environment are the managers of those missions operating?

Answer those questions and you'll watch your business grow like a mighty oak as you maximize your materials and resources.

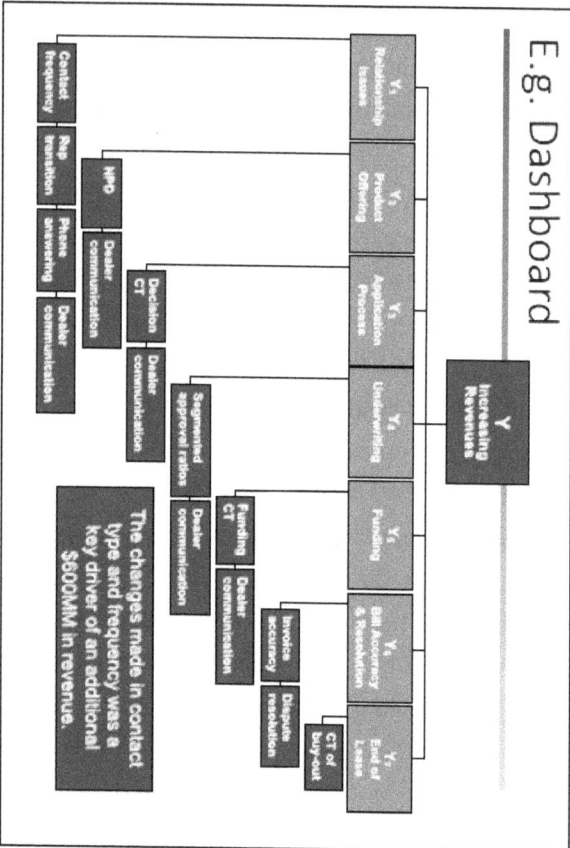

Figure 6: Sample dashboard linkages

Supply Chain Flow and Requirements

An oversupply of product costs you money, just as an undersupply can gnaw at the bottom line.

It's expensive and wasteful to store inventory solely for the sake of storing it—if there's no demand why make a product? But you also don't want to turn customers away because you can't service demand. So it is critical that we define clearly the objectives from both a manufacturing and marketing perspective.

But it doesn't stop there. The other piece that is just as important is supply flow chain and requirements. So what does that mean? As a manufacturer, you expect a constant supply of materials which your company assembles. So it's imperative you understand the flow of material from disparate parts and supplies to a market-quality product consumers want or need.

You can't take for granted that everything will be there. What are your redundancies or fail-safes? You should understand how long it takes for each supplier to get a specific part to you at an agreed-upon time at the right cost.

Similarly if you're providing services to a customer, chances are that client wants a certain value at a specific time for a budgeted cost. You need to understand how that value chain flows from your organization to your customer.

Curtain Call

Let's role play for a moment. Say you come up to us with this bright concept to sell to your customers. You've identified a customer group and you have identified a need. You have all the pricing marketing done. And you've told everybody about this new widget that you came up with. Matter of fact, you've stoked consumer demand so well that there's pent-up demand for a product customers have yet to even see.

Now let's talk about the supply chain. Assume that it takes 10 days to make this product. You can't basically wait till somebody places an order, the lag time would be too great.

Suddenly, you go from Day One with no sales to Day Six with demand going through the roof. What's your plan? Would this end as a comedy, a drama, or an epic of business success?

You may need to have some sort of ramped up plan for how you build your new product. This basically I'm calling it a P/P since the new product is being phased in as the old product is being phased out. That's important because you want to make sure that you don't short change your existing customers as you gradually transition them.

Customers may demand help for delivery, quality, returns, or whatever. You need to make sure you have support plans for maintaining the product.

That includes having resources identified and predefined for both customer support and product delivery.

Scoping it Out

We all need to have clear set of objectives and we also need to understand the scope of each area of the operations group in terms of what we are striving to do.

The first assumption you have to make is you can't do everything under the sun. You have finite resources so you need to have practical distribution and marketing area that serve as delineators of your scope—they narrow your vision to what's important to your business.

You need to make sure that if the operations group is targeting this market with this set of products then everybody understand that the scope of this operation is to basically get this product to this specific market within the time constraint defined by the market. Figure 7: *Sample Scope Elements For Operations Strategy*, highlights choices that can be targeted for execution excellence in order to maximize customer value.

One of key areas of oversight is initial shelve stock. I abbreviated it as ISS. You need to basically do your market assessment, do your promotion and based on your market assessment and the promotion define some amount balancing the risk of inventory.

Define some amount that you're going to pre-build and make available on day one to sell to your customers. That way, customer delivery time for the new products can be minimized.

The question is knowing that it costs money to pre-build, so you must determine how much inventory you can make and store without taking on undue financial exposure.

Strategy Formulation and Implementation

So if we start off with the strategic piece what does that mean? Well generally when it comes to strategy we're going to have to make choices. We can't do everything under the sun. So the question is what tactics are we going to employ in fighting the completion and which activities are we going to emphasize for excellence?

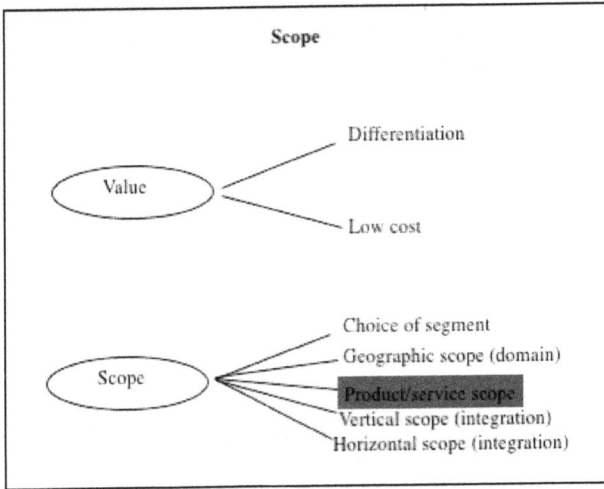

Figure 7: Sample scope elements for operations

In order to an actionable strategy, the following questions will need to be answered in order to define the scope of our market. The collective response from business stakeholders becomes the basis of operations strategy.

1. What business are you in?
2. What is your mission?
3. Who are your key customers?

Once you know the market and customer base you want to serve, you should asses your current strengths and weakness as well those of the environment in which your business will be operating. This insight can be achieved by doing

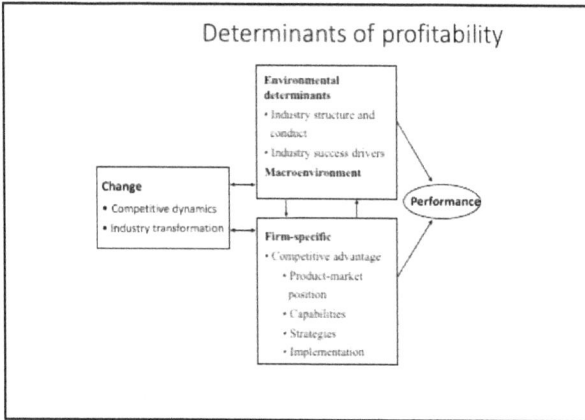

Figure 8: Sample levers of profitability

SWOT (Strengths, Weakness, Opportunities, and Threats) analysis, examining both internal operations and outside market factors.

With an understanding of your strengths and weakness, you can begin to identify the key strategic issues (KSI's) that your business needs to address to ensure its success.

Last but not least to the strategic framework is the roadmap to success. The elements of this roadmap are clear identification of the KSI's along with establishing metrics for measuring success and identifying initiatives to address KSI.

Understanding what drives profitability in the business (see Figure 8: *Sample Levers of Profitability*) can help assure that the right KSI's have been selected.

STRATEGIC OBJECTIVES				
LEADERSHIP Create robust diverse pipeline of extraordinary leaders		*GROWTH* Expand our worldwide leadership in devices and diagnostics		
FINANCIAL OBJECTIVES				
Top line revenue: (TBD) Net income: (TBD)				
STRATEGIC IMPERATIVES				
Build Extraordinary Leadership & Organizational Capabilities	Maximize WW DES Market Leadership	Drive Growth Outside Cardio DES	Drive Global Growth through Innovation and Market Creation	Ensure Global Operational Efficiency and Compliance Excellence
2008 AGENDA: KEY INITIATIVES				
1. Review critical leadership required to deliver priorities (PF)	1. Extend UBD (JH)	1. Successfully implement new Endo and Neuro organizational models (TBD)	1. Define market opportunity and develop key market models (TBD)	1. Enable new product approvals (TBD)
2. Enhance high performance culture (PF)	2. Launch line extensions (2.25/4.0, NxT, & Select Plus) (TK/VC)	2. Source innovation externally (TBD)	2. Align portfolio globally (TBD)	2. Lift FDA warning letter (TBD)
3. Define develop and implement diversity and inclusion strategy (PF)	3. Meet Neo critical project milestones (TK/VC)	3. Create Cordis incubators (e.g. NDC) (TBD)	3. Strengthen global collaboration (TBD)	3. Successfully implement new regulatory growth model for Endo (TBD)
4. Drive a culture of compliant, efficient growth (TBD)	4. Maximize DES portfolio for short and long term growth (PA)	4. Collaborate with other companies as a strategy (TBD)	4. Launch China pilot (TBD)	4. Lean out new product commercialization system (TBD)
	5. Expand claims, indications, and reimbursement (DD)	5. Accelerate innovation within Cordis (TBD)	5. Anticipate and shape the external environment (TBD)	5. Execute project Blazer (TBD)

Figure 9: Sample roadmap

With that behind you, all the elements can be assembled together as one guiding document (see Figure 9: *Sample Roadmap*).

Define your Future State

Growth rings in an oak tree are a sign of its age, as are other characteristics such as height or the spread of its branches. Likewise, your business must find ways to both measure progress toward its goals and make adjustments as needed. You need a combination then, of key milestones using sustainable improvement methods and specific guiding metrics to sustain gains achieved and build upon them.

The OAK principles provide a set of guiding principles that can be used by an organization to achieve strategic as well as operational excellence in the market place. These principles ensure that the flow of value to customers is continuously being improved and shareholders are getting their money's worth.

Let's See Your BCP

BCP means Business Continuity Plan. In a perfect world you come up with a plan and everything works well. Unfortunately, in the real world things don't always go according to plan so you need to have contingencies.

The BCP is sort of like our life preserver or lifeboat, it's how we can both save what we have and recoup to come back stronger.

What plans do you have to insure that you can continue delivering value to your customers in a calamity or an emergency?

A good example is the aftermath of those tragic events of Sept. 11, 2001. U.S. air space was shut down for a period of time.

Businesses with air supply chains were out of luck. Some firms, particularly in the auto parts industry, adapted quickly by switching to Plan B's that entailed over-the-road delivery of materials. Their backup plans also included alternative suppliers for critical components. So in those cases those businesses were able to basically retool with a backup plan and get things going quicker than enterprises that didn't have a plan.

The BCP Plan

What's your competitive edge? How quickly can your business adjust in the wake of a local emergency, national emergency?

Let's build our plan for business survivability with step-by-step process. The time to develop this plan and assemble all its components is in the early phases of implementation of the primary asset that needs to be protected.

In its simplest form, albeit likely to be most expensive, one can take out insurance on business operations. These programs typically can be structured to cover the loss of income in the event of a covered disaster. Unfortunately, there can be additional cost in the form of negative reputation and possibly market share loss when a business is not able to meet the needs of its customers with delivered goods and services.

A BCP plan not only preserves a company's revenue stream but also serve to provide continuity in the delivery of value (in the form of goods and services) to customers.

At a high level a good BCP action document addresses five key items:

1) Scope of the plan
2) Affected sites and processes
3) Failure mode and effects analysis
4) Contingencies and financial impact
5) Owners and modes of communication

Scope of the Plan

The scope of your BCP plan will typical line up with the scope of your operations plan. Generally, we are attempting to protect the goods and services that are coming out of a specific operation. As such, there is also a good estimate of potential revenue impact in the event of a disaster.

Affected Sites and Processes

Products and service delivery require resources to enable their delivery to customers. Understanding the full scope of what it takes to deliver specific products and services means knowing:

- Where they are produced,
- What processes are required,
- What inputs are needed,
- Where the inputs coming from (which suppliers),
- What technologies are required,

Failure Mode and Effect

In its extreme form a disaster can be so expansive as to cover all the affected sites and processes of a given scope of operations. On the other hand, impact could be limited to portions of the operations. The key is to understand how different disaster-related failures can occur and when they do, what their effect might show up as. One tool that is used often in this

Process Failure Mode and Effects Analysis Worksheet

	Process	Potential Failure Mode	Potential Effect(s) of Failure	Severity	Potential Cause(s) of Failure	Occurrenc	Current Controls	Detection	RPN	Recommended Action (use these actions to build the Control Plan)

Figure 10: Sample FMEA tool

assessment is the Failure Mode and Effect Analysis (FMEA) – see Figure 10: *Sample FMEA tool*.

To use the FMEA tool, you would start off with logical each element of your operations and analyze it for potential failure. Although, the failure analysis is typically done by process (hence the name), one can use it for any logical component with a beginning and an end.

The tool is most effective when done with a team in order to increase the likelihood of generating as many likely potential failure modes as possible from a diversity of perspective, experiences, and knowledge bases.

For each of the failure modes, you will then list the potential effect if it happens and the severity along with what might cause the failure. To prioritize development of potential mitigation solutions, the team will assign values for a) likelihood of occurrence and b) ability to detect failure. From these, one can compute a Risk Priority Number (RPN).

RPN = Severity * Detection * Occurrence

- **Severity (S)** - Severity is a numerical subjective estimate of how severe a customer will perceive the EFFECT of a failure.

- **Occurrence (O)** - Occurrence is a numerical subjective estimate of the likelihood that the cause of a failure mode will occur.

- **Detection (D)** - Detection is a numerical subjective estimate of the effectiveness of current controls to prevent or detect the failure mode before the failure reaches the customer. The assumption is that the cause has occurred.

Based on Severity and RPNs, prioritize which risk items need mitigation or contingency plans developed keeping in my mind cost versus benefit. Usually high Severity items will be addressed first. Regardless, of the timing of contingency action plans, an OAK resource must be assigned both for the implementation of the contingency as well as the operational execution of the plan.

4: OPERATIONS EXCELLENCE: Sustaining and Improving Performance

You can't flourish in the business of providing products or services to your customers by thinking you're going to do it the same way for ever and ever

Standing still is not an option because you'll be overtaken. You've got competition out there, other people that are coming up with new ideas. So you need to make sure that as part of running your business operations you have a mechanism to drive continuous improvement, to continuously delight your customers. Have the product present a better value to your customers with each incremental improvement opportunity.

Your business must have the mechanisms in place to drive continuous improvement. You should expect incremental improvement, but that's not enough. In fact, it's easy to be lulled into false comfort by a gradually rising bottom line. There's a tendency to reduce R&D, to see success as almost fore-ordained, and to lose sight of your vision.

That's why innovation is important. Only through pure luck or innovation can we open new markets or come up with new ideals to organically grow the business.

So innovation is going to be the third leg in making sure that we have a rhythm, a mechanism to keep all of your team on the same wavelength. You don't want some part of the business moving left as others are moving right, we want to all be aligned. All three of these elements—strategy, continuous improvement, and innovation—must support each other; your job is to make sure that synergy and synthesis is up and running every day.

The Eight Steps

What's your competitive edge? How do you sustain it? The knowledge to drive a culture of continuous improvement goes hand in hand with Ownership and Accountability within the OAK set of principles. This knowledge is integrated into the organization's people resources and the tools at their disposal. This is where a focus on tools training can

Getting Started – 8 Step Process

Step	Output
1. Identify Customers	COPIS
2. Establish Vision, Strategies and Goals	Road Map
3. Develop Customer Requirements	Completed COPIS
4. Metric Tracking	Dashboard, Control Tower
5. Define Processes	COPIS, Standard Work, Impact Maturity
6. Standardize, Analyze, & Execute	Standard Work, OPS Excellence Tool Kit, RRCA
7. How Are You Doing – Review Metrics, Vision, Strategy	Control Tower, QCPC, RRCA
8. Achieving Results	Mistake Proofing, CFA

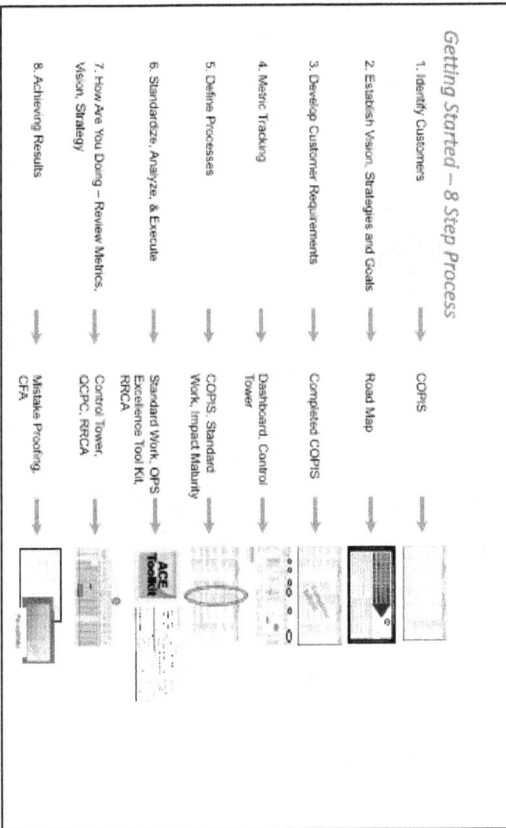

Figure 11: Eight Steps to Operations Excellence

help strengthen the Knowledge element of the OAK principles.

Your business exists by obtaining resources and training employees in how to use those materials with certain tools to deliver a specific product (or service) at an agreed-upon price that leaves a profit.

If you do that consistently, delighting the customer at each opportunity, you drive continuous improvement – this is operations excellence in a nutshell. Figure 11: *Eight Steps to Operations Excellence,* show the key set of steps and some of the tools required to achieve operations excellence.

The 8 step journey is a continuous journey (although it's laid out in a linear fashion in this figure for the sake of readability). As I have previously emphasized earlier in this book, it should go without saying that the OAK fundamentals of OWNERSHIP, ACCOUNTABILITY METRICS, and KNOWLEDGE —which will in part be addressing with a review of some tools in this section, are pre-requisites for a successful journey.

Knowing your customer, customer segments, and the value proposition that attracts them is a necessary first step. Operations excellence starts and ends with the customer. The customer is the reason why we are in business—they pay the bills. This insight will allow us to:

1. Focus on their (customers) needs and goals.
2. Anticipate the (customers) needs.
3. Deliver innovative value-added solutions.
4. Deliver products and services on time and error-free.
5. Retain profitable customers.

The customer experience is typically influenced by all functions of the organization (to varying degrees). Nonetheless, it is important that the value delivery processes within the business work together to deliver a consistently good experience for the customer. After all they only see one business unit (that has different parts to it). The flow of information and material that is required to meet the needs of customers is the value stream.

Generally the value stream (see Figure 12: Sample Value Stream Map) is characterized by the following:

1. The value stream starts and ends with the customer. The needs of customers define and dictate the organization's priorities. Work activities are setup with the goal of meeting customer expectations, even when the business unit has no direct contact with the purchaser of the product.

2. The outputs of one organization become the inputs of the next organization in the value stream. Therefore, the quality of work in one area directly affects the quality of work in other areas, as well as on the product or service delivered to the customer.

3. Within the organization, every entity is both a customer and a supplier

4. Internal customer-supplier relationships are just as important as relationships with external customers.
    Maximum value is attained when flow through the value stream is seamless and there is no waste from rework or rejects.

With the customer in focus, ensuring that there is a clear operations strategy becomes an essential element toward establishing a common destination and purposes for all the resources in the value chain.

The strategy roadmap document often will highlight the key initiatives, success factors and measurable goals for delivering value to customers. Again each element of the strategy will have an OAK to ensure it gets done. All too often it is not uncommon to see different functions of an organization get into the blame game when there is a miss on a strategic goal, hence the importance of an OAK. A simple tool for developing insight into value streams and supplier-customer relationships is the COPIS. In some circles, it is also referred to as the SIPOC.

Once all the customer types (and customer segments) have been identified, the next step is to define their key requirements and success criteria for delivering value to them. This can be done for internal as well as external customers. Additionally, requirements may not always show up as traditional quality specifications but could include elements of finance/cost as well as delivery. As a result process and resources may need to be setup to ensure any number of requirements are fulfilled including:

- Competitive pricing
- Optimized time and workflow
- Minimized setup and preparation time
- High availability level of equipment
- Knowing how customer is expecting to be satisfied
- Be able to track progress
- Solving problems quickly and effectively
-

Metrics tracking can be done using the dashboard tool. Once we know the deliverables that customers expect, they will need to be translated into specifics metrics for quality, delivery and cost. Some of the questions that will need to be answered to arrive at the appropriate metrics may include:

- What makes customers delighted?
- How do those things impact the business?

Standardize the delivery of value through the value stream to account for the metrics defined. This means that non-essential items that have no impact need to be taken off the radar.

It is important however that stakeholders be consulted before discarding a previously established requirement. Once deliverables and goals have been establish, they need to be transferred into process requirements. By integrating these requirements into the process itself, it assures consistency in delivery at each opportunity. Although customers typically purchase goods and services, shareholders and investors are also customers.

They spend money with the expectation of returns. As such, when we talk about defining customer requirements it is important that all customer needs be considered. This means that traditional product or service customer requirements needed to be balance against business constraints that affect shareholders (e.g. headcount, capital expenditures, profit margins, etc.). The dashboard provides a mechanism to track a balance set of metrics that track all competing customer requirements.

Standardizing the processes for delivering value to customers is a necessary prerequisite for delivering consistency. Customers have expectation of quality and expect to get them with every opportunity. This means understanding what the key processes are that affect the delivery of value, and knowing the health of those key processes. A good world-class stable process typically has the following attributes:

- Has a defined process owner
- A standard method for running process
- Process is not reason for any known customer complaint
- Systematic mechanisms exist to continuously improve the standard work
- Process metrics are continuously monitored to identify improvement opportunities for action

Establish an operation rhythm for the business to review dashboard results together with business performance goals. This means all key stakeholders and OAKs understand performance expectations, goals, and timeline for achieving and meet periodically to assess progress and correct course as necessary.

The COPIS tool provides the framework for the eight steps reviewed above. It is fairly easy to assemble.

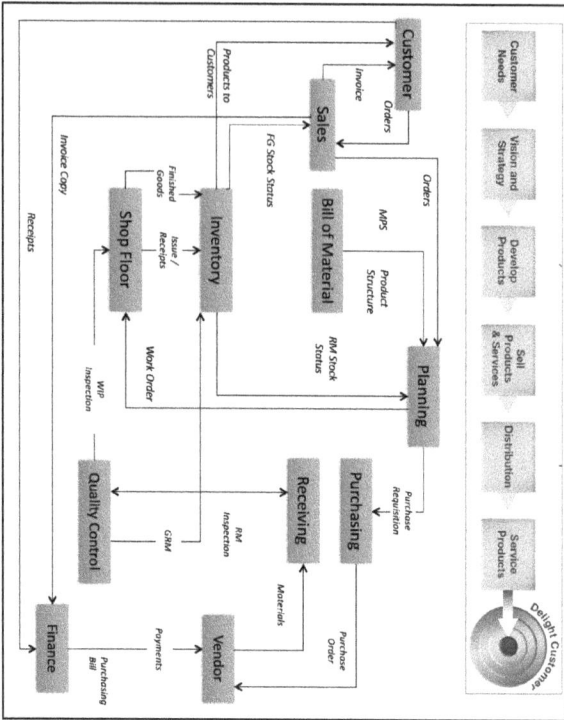

Figure 12: Sample Value Stream

First, you need SME's or Subject Matter Experts to lay out the process flow. A particular process SME could also be the process owner (but not always necessary). A process step must always have an owner that's accountable or that has the knowledge for the processes. Now the owner doesn't necessarily have to be the subject matter expert because the subject matter is really somebody that just knows their stuff technically. They just know it and the owner can rely on them for expertise. The process owner is accountable for whether the ship is sailing smooth or sinking.

What's a COPIS?

COPIS goes way back to the days of Six Sigma at GE when Jack Wells was running General Electric.

It's an acronym that means Customers, Outputs, Process, and Inputs and Suppliers. If you look at the chart below (see Figure 13: *COPIS Tool* and Figure 15: *Basic Process*). We can start off with the middle section called process.

In its simplest form, a process is a collection of activities that consumes resources in order to transform a set of inputs into outputs for the benefit of another process or end user.

IDENTIFY CUSTOMER REQUIREMENTS AND BUSINESS STRATEGY
COPIS TOOL

A. Customer	B. Outputs			C. Process	D. Inputs		E. Supplier	F. OAK
	B1. Description	B2. Delivery - Quantified measure	B3. Quality - Quantified measure		D1. Description	D2. Quantified measure		

A. Name(s) of customer(s): person, or organization that receives the output of the process

B. List of outputs (deliverables): customers expect from the process

B1. Qualitative description of outputs (deliverables). Not Applicable (N/A), where appropriate

B2. Quantitative measure of outputs (deliverables). Not Applicable (N/A), where appropriate

B3. Quantitative measure of outputs (deliverables). Not Applicable (N/A), where appropriate

C. Process that is necessary to produce the product or service (deliverable).

D. List of inputs (materials or information), received from suppliers, which are used to perform the process

D1. Qualitative description of inputs. Not Applicable (N/A), where appropriate

D2. Quantitative measure of inputs. Not Applicable (N/A), where appropriate

E. Name(s) of supplier(s) of information or materials used in this process.

F. OAK: Owner that is accountable for the success and operational stability of the process step

Figure 13: COPIS tool

Expectation of a process is that it will consistently deliver the expected output so long as the inputs and resources remain consistent - you put in something, you massage it and then out comes the expected output. A process could also have several sub-process embedded in it. For example a typical process for procuring and paying for goods might entail several sub-processes (see Figure 16: *High Level Procurement to Payment Process*).

Now let's get back to the COPIS. The way the COPIS table is set up is every process is going to have an input that comes in –that's raw materials and so forth. You have suppliers providing the inputs that go into the process and the process then is providing an output that is going to go to a customer.

So that is where you get the COPIS concept. It's very important because you need to know your customers, you need to know what is important to them and that is where the outputs comes in and then you also need to know your inputs and you need to know who your suppliers are that are providing the inputs.

Then the next step, item number 4, is defining standard work for each process.

The COPIS tool can be used for both internal sub-processes as well external facing processes.

Customers (e)	Outputs (d) Description (d1)	Quantified measure Quality(d3)	Process (c)	Inputs (b) Description (b1)	Quantified measure (b2)	Suppliers (a)
Vendor, Employee	Purchase order, price, delivery date		**Ordering Goods / Services** Request via Requisition Generate PO Send to Vendor	Purchase requisition		Employees
Purchasing, Branch	Goods received against PO in ERP	Correct quantity. Correct item received. Correct freight. Timely receipt in ERP	**Receiving Goods / Services** Confirm shipping slip/serv. Receipt to ERP	Packing slip		Receiving department Warehouse
Finance	Payable logged in ERP	Payment to correct vendor. Reference correct invoice. Correct $ amount.	**Process Invoice** Match invoice to PO, Receipt Voucher invoice Submit Payment Proposal	Invoice GL Coding / Receipt Approval		Vendor AP
Finance Vendor	Invoice released in ERP for payment.	Reference to invoice# Correct account # Correct invoice date	**Cheque Run** Review & print chk. Get >10K approval Scan & mail chk.	Payment proposal in ERP		AP
Vendor, Employee	Cheque	N/A	**Payment of Invoice**	Cheque run listing		AP

Figure 14: Basic view of a process

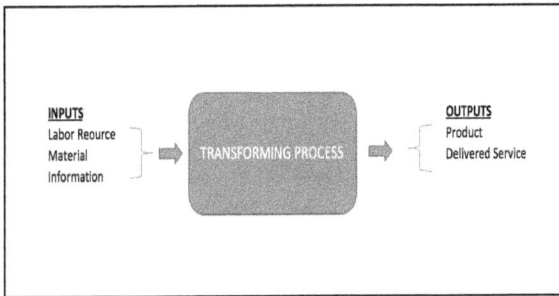

Figure 15: Basic process

process is a set of tasks or activities that you do to basically get an expected result. Because it's a process it basically happens day in day out. You can't do it one way today or another way tomorrow and call it a process. Customers have expectations in terms of what the product is supposed to do for them. In order to deliver to those expectations you need to do it the same way consistently. Defining the standard or the standard method for processing that thing is very important.

Step five entails ensuring each step of the process has been reviewed with the OAK. The owner, the person that's accountable, has to have a stake in it. You must review the process with them and give them the opportunity to have a sense of ownership in it. Get their input (this is where you bring in the warehouse people, the marketers) and make sure everybody is aligned.

Once you achieve that alignment engagement you can move to the next step of making sure you manage and control the process. Two things that are critical. One is a definition of how you do it today. The other piece is an acknowledgement that you're going to improve your operation tomorrow— if not sooner!

You solicit feedback to help plan improvements. So we need to have mechanisms for making changes in order to improve the process. Having standardization and consistency doesn't

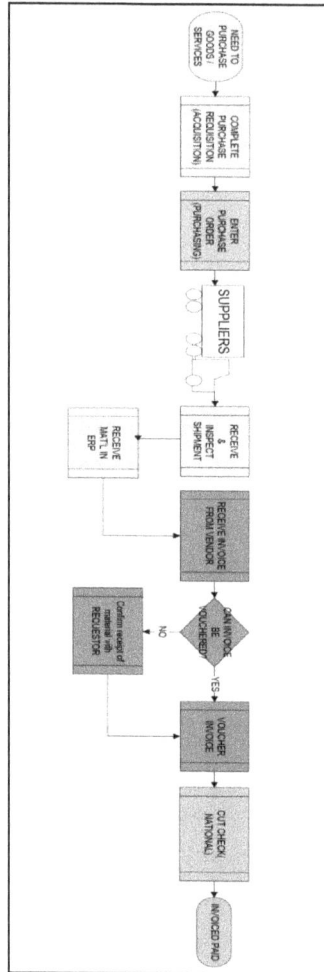

Figure 16: High level procurement to payment process

mean that a process cannot be improved. It just means that we need to do control changes.

Consider software updates that you get on your phone. Typically vendors develop software changes based on issue or customers feedback or marketing opportunities. They then make sure they test it with a small group. In some cases they would actually use real customers but a smaller subset and piloted.

Once they resolve key issues based on customer input, they roll it out to the rest of the customer base. So essentially they are acknowledging that they need to make changes but are opting to incorporate changes into their release products in a controlled fashion.

.

When Companies Collide

Back in the late 1980's Liquid Crystal Display (LCD) glass was beginning to emerge as an alternative to traditional cathode ray tube (CRT) used in making television.

CRT had been around since the advent television. A multi-billion company that supplied CRT to all major TV manufacturers was aggressively working to develop its process for making LCD. But time was running out as other glass manufacturers had entered the market and were producing very good CRT. The company's last remaining CRT manufacturing site had just received letters from Sony and Phillips electronics threatening to sever ties if quality did not improve within 2 to 4 months.

The combined volume of sales represented more that 70% of the plant's yearly output. The loss of these customers would definitely mean the closure of the facility and jeopardize the company's ability to transition their customers to LCD when it became commercially ready.

The company decided to bring back from retirement one of their executives who had help developed a highly successful process discipline program in another division in the past. This new plant manager initiated a couple of programs immediately.

The first program was focused on simplifying their product mix. It turned out in their quest to make customers happy their sales team was selling every possible option and size configuration to customers. The resulting variety of tooling and process setup standards were overwhelming the facility and leading to multitude of mistakes and other quality related issues.

Keep It Simple

So SKU simplification and reduction became a goal. By reducing the number of product types and sizes by 25% they were able to cut quality issues in excess of 50%. Even after they reduced SKUs by 50% they were able to retain same volume of sales.

The second aspect of the program focused on process standards—ensuring that processes had defined bogey standards and were run to those standards. This requirement alone reduced significantly the need for process engineers to continuous troubleshoot and the process to maintain quality.

Today companies like Apple place a premium on simplification, standardizing on a few product configurations in and optimizing design, quality, and cost on those products. This is very evident in the smartphone market when you compare the number of iPhone SKUs versus that of android phone manufacturer such as Samsung.

The value of simplicity cannot be over emphasized. Conversely, complexity can be an expensive unwanted state that should be avoided as much as possible. This means aspiring to clean, uncluttered work environment with straightforward work standards. This also means each process area needs to be standardized for simplicity, analyze for complexity reduction, and improved to deliver better value. There are numerous process improvement tools in use today to accomplish these goals but a few key ones that tend to have universal application are the following:

5S – For Establishing Order in the Work Environment

5S promotes a visual and efficient workplace environment that puts all items in their defined locations and storage points.

How to:

1. Sort:
   - Establish sort areas in the workplace.
   - Identify items to keep, items to reuse, items to throw away.
   - Label supplies
   - Take pictures to establish baseline record.
   - Gather team and communicate expectations,
   - Eliminate what is not needed.
   - Keep items that support your business.
2. Straighten
   - Organize what remain using visual controls.
   - Put items labeled from previous (Sort) step in labeled area.
   - Ensure items are in order and can be easily accessed.
3. Shine:
   - Make problems visible so they can be addressed.

- Clean to make inspection easier.
- Inspect to correct and improve performance.

4. Standardize:
   - Define standard work for cleaning and maintenance.
   - Get buy-in from all stakeholders including staff and management.
   - Communicate the standard work and make it a way of running the work place.

5. Sustain
   - Implement the standard work as a process with identified OAK.
   - Monitor progress by scheduling and performing regular intervals of assessments.
   - Drive continuous improvements and update standard work.

The resulting workplace environment from an effective 5S program typically has the additional attributes of a workplace that is safe, refreshing, and self-improving.

Value Stream Process Management (VSPM)

VSPM provides a structured method for identifying waste within a process, and improving them through standardization.

1. Identify Customer requirements and business strategy
   - What are the key product families?
   - What are the daily customer demands by product?

2. Product Process Flow
   - How long does a typical unit of the product or service flow through the operations as evidenced through video recording?
   - As a percent of the total throughput time of the product what is the portion of actual value-added time?
   - What portion of the total throughput time is related to Storage of the product?
   - What portion of the total throughput time is related to transporting the product?
   - What portion of the total throughput time is related to inspecting the product?

- What portion of the total throughput time is related to other non-value-added activities?

3. Labor Analysis
   - Identify operations process step to be analyzed.
   - Video tape selected operation from the beginning of one part processing to the beginning of a second part processing.
   - Analyze Labor walk pattern to identify stray walks that can be eliminated.
   - Analyze labor time to identify idle times that can be eliminated.
   - Develop work station layout maximize value-added activities.
   - Identify and categorize improvement ideas.

4. Develop Standard Work
   - Define standard work to maximize value-added time.
   - Incorporate improvement ideas from labor and product-process flow analysis.

5. Performance Measures
   - Define metrics for tracking performance of the operations.
   - Define standards for each metric.
   - Establish rhythm for performance review.

- Identify opportunities for improvement and implement corrective actions.

Setup Reduction for Reducing Idle Time

Setup reduction provides a methodical processes for reducing the amount of time it takes a resource to change over from one good piece (of product) run to the first good piece of the next run.

1. Analyze current process
   - Analyze current state to determine scope and capacity requirements.
   - Video tape and analyze current process to document sequence of steps.
   - Classify setup activities into Internal (activities performed while machine is shutdown) versus External (activities performed while equipment is operating).
2. Eliminate obvious waste
   - Identify typical causes of setup delays and waste.
   - Develop corrective actions for setup waste.
3. Move Internal to External

- Focus on moving internal setup activities to external.
- Focus on reducing external setup activity time.
- Use planning, pre-kitting actions to eliminate waste.
- Conduct practice runs to standardize.

4. Simplify, Standardize, Implement and Monitor
   - Create standard work for changeover.
   - Modify, standardize job aids and tools.
   - Communicate and train to standard.

OPERATIONS EXCELLENCE TOOLS - QUICK REFERENCE GUIDE (1 OF 2)

TOOL	GENERIC EXPLANATION	GENERAL STEPS TO IMPLEMENT	PERSONAL EXAMPLE
Process Improvement and Waste Elimination			
1. 5S	Place for everything and everything in its place	1. Sort 2. Straighten 3. Shine 4. Standardize 5. Sustain	• Quickly find tools and material in a garage. • Quickly locate paperwork in a filing cabinet
2. Value Stream Process Management (VSPM)	Quality and flow optimization, mature and high-impact processes	1. Identify Customer Requirements and Business Strategy 2. Product Process Flow 3. Labor Analysis 4. Standard Work 5. Setup Reduction 6. Performance Measure	• Know what works the fastest and smoothest to get the most production out of your day. • Know how many people to schedule for a given production run at the lowest cost.
3. Standard Work	Reduce variability	1. Identify Type of Standard Work 2. Create/Modify Documents 3. Communicate Changes 4. Verify Use	Each member of your family folds laundry and stores the different items the same way.
4. Production Preparation Process (3P)	Revolutionary change strategy	1. Determine 3P Purpose 2. Brainstorm Design Ideas 3. Decide on Designs 4. Conduct Experiments/Trials 5. Select Best Designs	Design landscaping (includes location of shed) before the first seed is planted
5. Total Production Maintenance (TPM)	Reliable equipment	1. Identify and Categorize Equipment 2. Clean Equipment 3. Eliminate Sources of Contamination 4. Establish Standards 5. Implement and Monitor	Schedule lawnmower oil and gas checks so it is always ready when you need it
6. Setup Reduction	Get up and go	1. Analyze Current Process 2. Eliminate Obvious Waste 3. Move Internal to External 4. Simplify and Standardize 5. Implement and Monitor	Put the garden hose reel to water the garden near the spigot (versus shed/garage)
7. Process Certification	Variability reduction & management; Data driven decision making	1. Form Team 2. Define Process 3. Review and Access 4. Establish Control 5. Develop Control Plan 6. Certify Process	Assure the volume of water used to maintain the health of the landscape is consistent at every interval

Figure 17A: Sample operations excellence tools (2 of 2)

OPERATIONS EXCELLENCE TOOLS - QUICK REFERENCE GUIDE (1 OF 2)

Process Improvement and Waste Elimination

TOOL	GENERIC EXPLANATION	GENERAL STEPS TO IMPLEMENT	PERSONAL EXAMPLE
1. 5S	Place for everything and everything in its place	1. Sort 2. Straighten 3. Shine 4. Standardize 5. Sustain	• Quickly find tools and material in a garage. • Quickly locate paperwork in a filing cabinet.
2. Value Stream Process Management (VSPM)	Quality and flow optimization; mature and high-impact processes	1. Identify Customer Requirements and Business Strategy 2. Product Process Flow 3. Labor Analysis 4. Standard Work 5. Setup Reduction 6. Performance Measure	• Know what works the fastest and smartest to get the most production out of your day • Know how many people to schedule for a given production run at the lowest cost.
3. Standard Work	Reduce variability	1. Identify Type of Standard Work 2. Create/Modify Documents 3. Communicate Changes 4. Verify Use	Each member of your family folds laundry and stores the different items the same way.
4. Production Preparation Process (3P)	Revolutionary change strategy	1. Determine 3P Purpose 2. Brainstorm Design Ideas 3. Decide on Designs 4. Conduct Experiments/Trials 5. Select Best Designs	Design landscaping (includes location of shed) before the first seed is planted.
5. Total Production Maintenance (TPM)	Reliable equipment	1. Identify and Categorize Equipment 2. Clean Equipment 3. Eliminate Sources of Contamination 4. Establish Standards 5. Implement and Monitor	Schedule lawnmower oil and gas checks so it is always ready when you need it
6. Setup Reduction	Get up and go	1. Analyze Current Process 2. Eliminate Obvious Waste 3. Move Internal to External 4. Simplify and Standardize 5. Implement and Monitor	Put the garden hose reel to water the garden near the spigot (versus shed/garage)
7. Process Certification	Variability reduction & management. Data driven decision making	1. Form Team 2. Define Process 3. Review and Access 4. Establish Control 5. Develop Control Plan 6. Certify Process	Assure the volume of water used to maintain the beauty of the landscape is consistent at every interval.

Figure 17B: Sample operations excellence tools (1 of 2)

5: CORPORATE ENTREPRENUERSHIP / OPERATIONAL INNOVATION

The Linkage with Operational Excellence

We've previously covered the concept of operation strategy and operations excellence. The basic premise here is that in order for us to be successful at delivering value to customers we need to define clearly strategic goals and objectives. As part of the strategic objectives we also need to make sure that we have the operational roadmap with the appropriate metrics to get us to those set of objectives. The metrics help us track progress so we can assure we are moving in the right direction.

Now in this discussion there are a set of assumptions that we need to make sure are in place for any of these concepts that we're talking about to be successful. So what are these assumptions?

Generally the Oak concept requires 3 elements to be in place:

- Ownership Culture
- Accountability Metrics
- Knowledge to get the job done

These elements typically serve to provide consistent delivery of products and services to customers that over time get better with gradual continuous improvements. Unfortunately, in a connected global world of commercial competition, **innovation** is needed to infuse a bolt of energy in the improvement trajectory once in a while, in order to stay ahead. This is where operational innovation and corporate entrepreneurship comes in.

Operational innovation means coming up with entirely new ways of developing products, delivering value-added services to customers, or doing any other activity that an enterprise performs. In essence, it is corporate entrepreneurship at an enterprise level.

We are now going to focus our attention on driving operational innovation through corporate entrepreneurship.

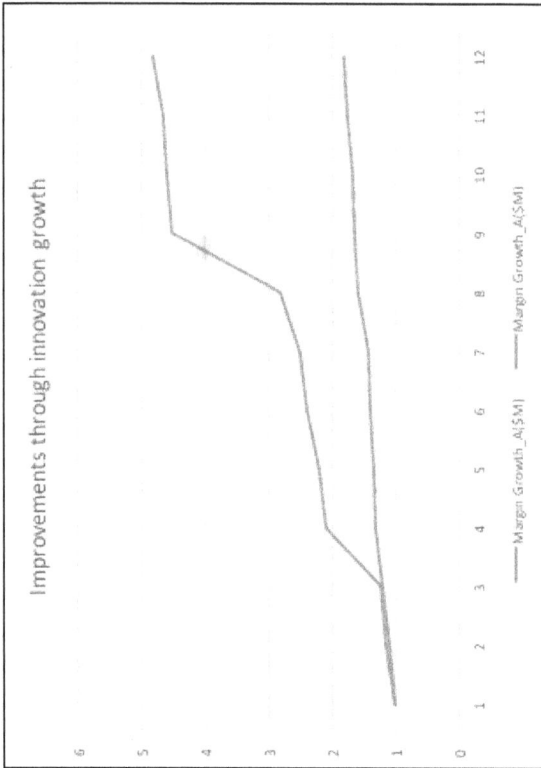

We will discuss the entrepreneurial activities that we need to bring to the table to help us deliver step changes and improvements in the way we do things or in the way we do business. How does operational innovation link to the whole concept of continuous improvement?

Figure 18: Achieving gains through innovation and continuous improvement.

The Dynamics of Change

If you refer to the diagram in Figure 18, continuous improvement would manifest itself as a gradual positive change over time in the value that gets delivered to customers. These could be in terms of product price, cycle time, quality, or functionality. Over time, incremental step changes will come about as we innovate and allow us to deliver significantly higher value to customers. Continuous improvement typically relies on existing modes of operation to reduce costs, errors, and cycle time in order to achieve higher performance. The fundamentals of how work is accomplished remain the same.

Operational Innovation

In contrast to your continuous operational improvement, operational innovation means inventing and deploying new ways of doing work within the enterprise. When we talk about innovation, it typically manifests itself as a step change in terms of the value that we're delivering to our customers. Let's now discuss innovation and what it really means. Innovation can take multiple forms. So let's look at three examples.

In the first example we're talking about the creation of new things. Here we are looking at entering new markets with new ideas, products, or services. We could also be looking at greenfield opportunities where we start a whole new enterprise or supply chain from scratch.

Another example where we create new things might be in the form of scenario planning or futuring on an idea that has never been previously introduced. So that's basically talking about new things when it comes innovation.

A Passage to Mali

The second type of innovation might be one where we look for ways of doing things in a more robust fashion. What does that mean? It means things like efficiency improvements, supply chain innovations, quality improvements, or expanded usage and application of an existing item.

In this particular context, we may be talking about creative ideas that allow us to make things more efficient, faster, or higher quality. We may be talking about something that previously took a long cycle time to complete, and through innovation significantly reducing the time by several orders of magnitude. A hypothetical example might be the act of getting a visa to visit another country.

Let's say in order to get a visa to visit Mali you have to send your passport in along with your visa application to get a stamp. Let's assume further that it takes two weeks to get it back after they receive it. Now if somebody came up with an innovative Internet-based visa stamp process, you could conceivable apply for the visa over the internet, get it approved so you can print and affix it to your passport.

Of course, since this is hypothetical, we can assume the innovation addresses all relevant security and quality issues related to the visa granting process but the point is that such an innovation, were it to occur will significantly reduce the cycle time for getting a visa.

Figure 19: *Operations Excellence Tools*, shows examples of some of the key improvement tools that can be used by an organization.

Don't Procrastinate

Doing things NOW is another mechanism for innovation. For example, a crisis needs to be resolved quickly and creativity is often required.

A less imperative scenario of doing things NOW may involve market adjacencies, where one takes an existing product or service and finds an application in an adjacent market. This can happen in the pharmaceutical industry when a drug that is previously approved for a particular treatment is

OPERATIONS EXCELLENCE TOOLS – QUICK REFERENCE GUIDE (2 OF 2)

TOOL	GENERIC EXPLANATION	GENERAL STEPS TO IMPLEMENT	PERSONAL EXAMPLE
Problem Solving			
8. Customer Feedback Analysis (CFA)	Am I doing what is needed	Define Customer and Metrics Collect Feedback Analyze Feedback Resolve Problems Monitor Feedback	Verify with other home residents that particular "green thing" are weeds and not plants Make sure that your definition of upkeep is the same as other home residents
9. Quality Clinic Process Charting (QCPC)	Mistakes	Initiate QCPC System Collect and Sort Data Analyze Data Prioritize Project List Document Success	Mowed over what appeared to be plants two times over the past two months Lawnmower had no gas twice this month
10. Relentless Root Cause Analysis (RRCA)	Address root problem	Define Problem/Projects Investigate Process Verify Solution Ensure Improvement	Cannot distinguish between weeds or plants Basement flooding recurs even after waterproofing the basement.. oops, the gutter downspout is broken
11. Mistake Proofing	Ensure it does not happen again		Separate plants and lawn with a fence Put new no-clog gutters and downspouts to prevent future basement floods
Decision Making			
12. Passport Process	Stay on the right track	Select Passport Board Identify Gates Complete Work Present to Passport Board Receive Passport Board Decision	Landscaper plans, designs, and creates new garden and lawn before homeowner's party. Landscaper regularly gets feedback from homeowner at each building phase to ensure it meets the homeowner's requirements.
Best In Class			
Benchmarking	Get up and go	Collect Baseline Data Develop Questions Research Best-in-Class Select Partners Collect Partner Information Implement and Monitor	You find the best lawns in the neighborhood, then you ask those neighbors how they take care of the lawn because it looks thick and green. You adopt the methods that are best suited to your budget and schedule.

Figure 19: Sample operations excellence tools (2 of 2)s

found to have efficacy in an adjacent application or market.

Root cause analysis and problem solving in general provide another example of doing things now to innovate. So you have a problem that you need to solve. Conducting root cause analysis to determine cause of an underlying problem and developing solutions can certainly bring out the creativity in individuals to solve those problems.

Benefits of Innovation:

Operational innovation has delivered significant business results to a number of companies over the last century or so in just about every industry. Typically, the enterprises that have successfully managed and commercialized innovations time after time are the ones that have profited tremendously. Said differently, organizations that do not sustain or manage entrepreneurship typically fail after one accidental success.

Notable companies with strong processes for managing innovation and entrepreneurism include 3M (with its history in Kevlar, nylon, adhesives, etc.), Google (search algorithms, autonomous navigation systems), Walmart's logistics systems, IT inventory and management methods, or Toyota with its lean manufacturing, total quality systems, etc.

At the enterprise level, innovation can lead to new sources of topline growth. It can ignite enthusiasm in your organization. It can avoid the diminishing return of gradual continuous improvement that is typical of continuous improvement. People get tired of seeing slow paced incremental improvements. Innovation helps reignite the spark in everybody.

Institutionalizing Innovation

As a quick recap we have discussed defining the value stream for your business and using continuous improvement tools to improve gradually all aspects of that value stream. We have also discussed how innovation allows the organization to build incrementally upon those improvements with significant step change improvements.

While continuous improvements activities tend to be part of the rhythm of the business operations, innovations on the other hand can be infrequent. They can sometimes even be replacement for existing value streams. As such, it is typically necessary to have organizational mechanisms in place to draw them out and nurture them to fruition. How do you that?

In a small organization it could be as simple as identifying an owner that is tasked with the responsibility of finding and generating new ideas. But in a large organization, that responsibility may be assigned to a team. In that context, it can be either Business Unit driven or a dedicated stand-alone team. Regardless of structure, the clear ownership and accountability for seeking out creative ideas is a critical foundation. The innovation owner once defined may employ different mechanisms and tools to assemble ideas for further development. These could be as simple as the following examples:

Look and Listen for Innovation

An idea collection system provides a mechanism for individuals to submit new ideas, or new opportunities for consideration. As an incentive they either get rewarded or recognized by the organization if their contribution is selected for further development. Typically, there will be a vetting mechanism or cross-functional vetting team that reviews the selections for subsequent development and funding.

Another mechanism could be the use of a customer/quality feedback collection process. In that case, the organization will have in place mechanism for collecting feedback from customers, both internal and external, as well as quality related issues. Once a week or periodically as appropriate, these will be reviewed for resolution. Once they are selected and prioritized, they will be assigned to small teams to conduct quick brainstorming sessions for potential solutions. The ideas generated can then become the basis for further refinement and development.

In another scenario, the team charged with innovation embarks on idea search events where they canvas conferences and specific venues to look for potential innovations. One can even go as far as hosting regular events, at which participants are sponsored or invited to present.

Get an Innovation Owner

Regardless of how the initial innovation ideas are collected or come across, the key is having a clear owner for the subsequent refinement and development of the initial ideas. In a technology company, it may be referred to as a Technology Assessment Committee (TAC) that will be charged with the selection, funding, and sponsorship of idea development initiatives.

Once an innovation idea has attained sufficient progress or clarity to merit achievable commercial potential, it needs to be manage more like a commercialization project. In other words, an innovation development phase needs to be distinct from a commercialization phase in order to ensure that ideas don't remain ideas in perpetuity. In a sense, it is like shooting a target.

Take That Shot

Refining your aim to increase your chances of success is important but you cannot be aiming forever. At some point you will need to go through the act of squeezing the trigger to take the shot. An idea that has been aimed thus needs to be moved into the next phase of squeezing the trigger for the shot. This is the commercialization phase. This is where it needs to have all the plans defined for the supporting operations including the supply chain, the technology, market support, etc.

In some technology companies this phase is managed by a Portfolio Action Committee (PAC) that is charged with funding, reviewing, and approving the milestone progressions in place for commercialization projects. They typically use a phase-review or stage-gate review process to balance risk management and speed to market.

Speeding Up Innovation While Minimizing Risk

We have discussed the importance of ensuring that someone is on point for running the innovation process. While this person owns the smooth running of the process, we cannot rely on their expertise and inputs only to shape ideas as they come along, nor

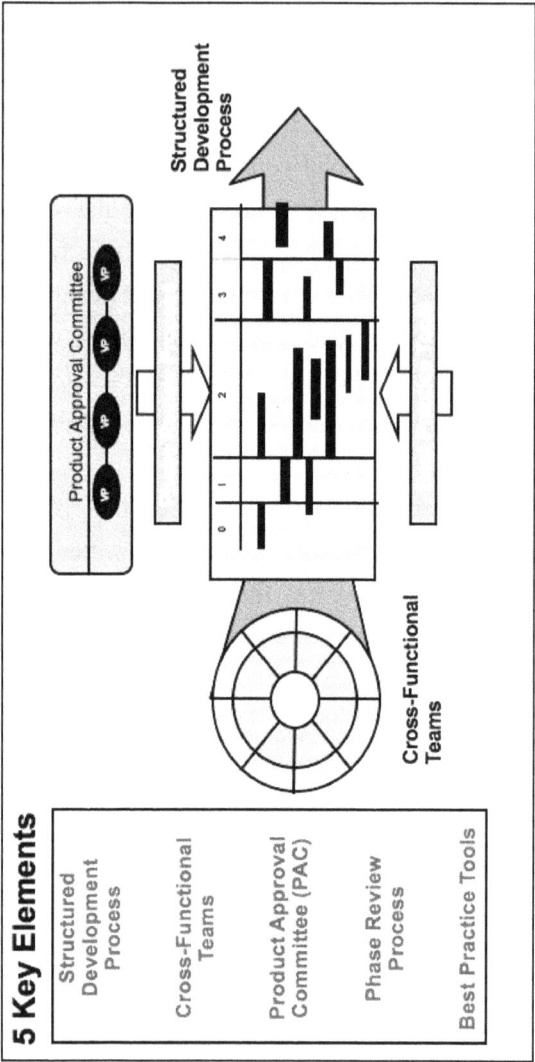

Figure 20: Phase gated review process for new product introduction

can the organization take input from every member (else things become very bureaucratic). The key is to identify key stakeholders in new products and services and making sure the mechanisms are in place to incorporate their inputs in the development of new ideas. Your stakeholders might include marketing, finance, operations, etc.

One common best practice process for managing and developing innovation ideas into commercial products and service is the phase gated review process (see Figure 20).

This process is typified by five key elements: a structured predefined roadmap, cross-functional stakeholder team, an approval committee, phase reviews, and use of best practices functional tools. There is a project leader for one or multiple program ideas who is supported by a cross-functional team as the core team.

While the core team itself may be supported as needed by an extended team, it alone is empowered to plan and lead product delivery from concept approval to commercialization and market launch. Core team has responsibility for achieving both technical goals and business success for the project.

Each core team member may additionally lead and extended team (as appropriate) working on the project. Figure 21: *Program Core Team Structure.*

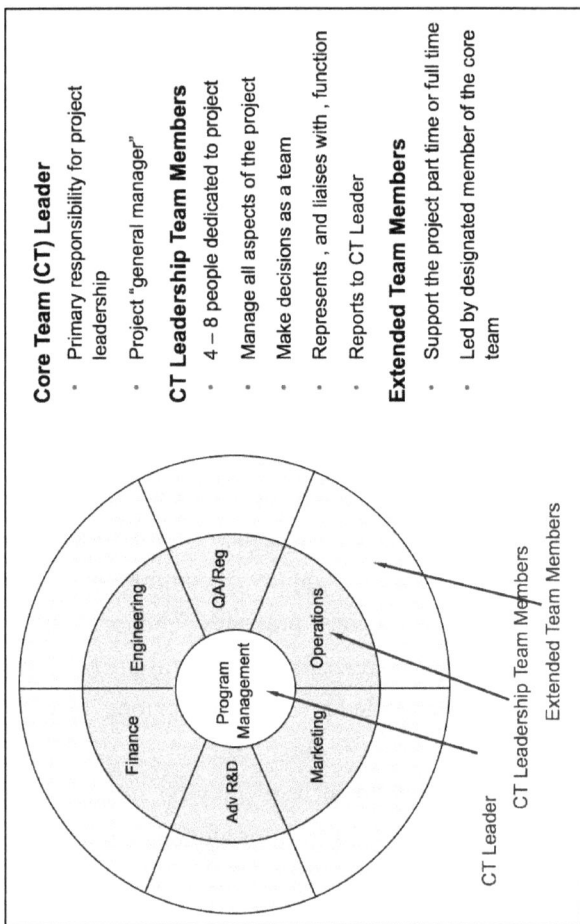

Core Team (CT) Leader

- Primary responsibility for project leadership
- Project "general manager"

CT Leadership Team Members

- 4 – 8 people dedicated to project
- Manage all aspects of the project
- Make decisions as a team
- Represents , and liaises with , function
- Reports to CT Leader

Extended Team Members

- Support the project part time or full time
- Led by designated member of the core team

CT Leader

CT Leadership Team Members

Extended Team Members

Program Management

QA/Reg

Engineering

Finance

Adv R&D

Marketing

Operations

Figure 21: Example project core team structure

shows an example of a team setup and role descriptions:

Project Team Leader leads the project to successful completion and:

- Acts as focal point for project communications and general manager of the project.
- Facilitate decision making to achieve optimum project results.
- Leader of project team consensus process and arbitrator of conflicts.
- Negotiator for project resources.
- Assist group become a high-performing team.

Core Team Member manages contributions from both their immediate functional area as well as the wider circle of groups they represent (e.g. their Extended Team(s)) and:

- Participate in core team decision making to achieve optimum project results.
- Liaison/spokesperson of project's functional group resources assigned by the functional manager.
- Communicator of issues and decisions to and from their own functional manager, and the extended team members.

- Facilitator of conflict resolution within functional area as it pertains to project.
- Ensure project gets adequate resource from own functional group to support project.
- Keeping the Core Team leader updated on progress, risks, and issues.

Extended Team Members help define their contributions and commitments, and perform tasks to meet those commitments. Additionally:

- Provide functional expertise (as appropriate).
- Plan and perform specific functional activities to support the project and review processes

Functional Managers, when it comes to product development, have the role of providing necessary resources and support for projects for which commitments have been made. They also have responsibilities for:

- Developing functional resource plans for new projects.
- Balancing resource allocation between projects and day to day functional activities.
- Providing the necessary skilled resources to fulfill project commitments.

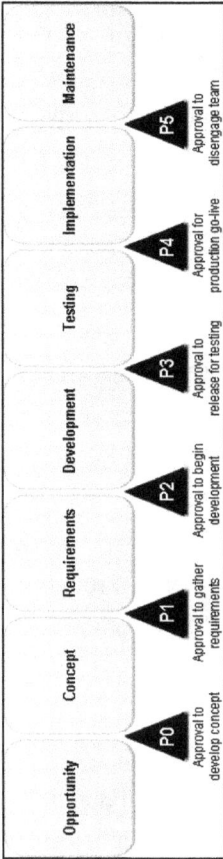

Figure 22: Typical phase-gated sequence

• Assuring that appropriate functional needs and tasks have been addressed by the team.

• Developing and maintaining functional expertise, tools, and infrastructure.

To summarize the phase gated review process, it must be noted that it's most appropriately used to improve decision-making capabilities for strategic activities— the kind that involve large scale transformations or programs.

Once an idea has been accepted for development, it will typically be resourced with a core team who would have responsibility for taking it through the phase gated process. Depending on the complexity and type of project, the gates may vary but a typical sequence is shown in Figure 21: *Typical phase-gated sequence*.

The gates in the process will typically be aligned to key project milestones with the intent to manage both risk and resources. At each phase gate review, one of three key decisions will be made along with appropriate relevant supporting actions. Such decision might reflect one of the following:

Go:
- Authorizes and empowers Project Team to proceed through the next phase based on clear performance goals in the next-phase contract
- Commits resources (people, capital, expenses, test facilities, etc.) through the next phase only

No Go:
- Applicable when the program:
- Does not meet a market requirement
- Is not technically feasible to develop
- Does not fit business strategy or risk/return criteria
- Requires resources beyond the capacity or capabilities of the organization

Redirect:
More data is needed to support the decision

Project Action Committee must provide the Project Team with specific guidance and time frame for a comeback

Some reasons for a no go decision could be that the project does not meet a market requirement, is not technically feasible to develop, does not fit the business strategy or risk-return criteria, or requires resources beyond the capacity or capabilities of the organization. Exit ramp strategies, or contingencies, should then be considered to extract residual value from terminations.

Idea Generation Tools to Stimulate Innovation

Having a process to manage innovation is key to the long-term growth of a business but being able to plant the seeds of innovation on a regular basis can be aided by well-known tools and techniques that have been around for some time. In the next few pages we will review some of these tools and their usage.

Creativity is one those human attributes that sometimes seems caged and afraid to come out. There are times when we have hit a road block on a project and need to come up with a breakthrough idea to get around it. These could be:

- Project constraints
- Resources limitations
- Budgets, etc.
- Limits of our own technical knowledge
- Mechanics, physical sciences, etc.
- No known way to deal with a particular problem
- Psychological inertia
- Result of life experiences
- Cultural backgrounds
- Staying in a comfort zone
- "This is how we've always done it" syndrome

Sometimes we can be our own worst enemies. Regardless of the roadblocks that may be facing us, understanding how obstacles hold our creative juices back can be a first step to developing mechanisms for stimulating it. Typical obstacles can include the following:

- Not challenging existing paradigms
- Not challenging assumptions
- Fear of being wrong
- Early childhood and school experiences
- The search for the "right" answer
- Focusing on logical thought
- Judging ideas before they are formed

- Psychological inertia
- Solutions Based Logic

When kids can't solve a problem they cry. When adults can't solve a problem, they compromise. Sometimes you can't cry or compromise your way out of a challenge. You have to uncage your creativity and bring a whole new paradigm to finding solutions. Here are three common tools for forcing idea generation followed by brief explanations.

Brainstorming Steps

1. Clearly state the purpose of the Brainstorming session
2. Select Recorder(s) to capture ideas on flipcharts.
3. Call out ideas in a round robin style (each person gets a turn, going around the group - it's OK to Pass):

    - Don't discuss or criticize ideas; often ideas from left field are the most useful
    - Build on ideas of others. Listen to the others' ideas; you may be inspired!
    - A variation of brainstorming asks each member to write ideas down before the session

- When the round robin has slowed down, open the brainstorming session up to any additional ideas.
- When the brainstorm has ended, review the list. Clarify the remaining ideas (add additional words) making sure that everybody understands each idea. Delete any duplicate ideas.

Challenge Assumptions

Everyone brings assumptions to the problem-solving table. Such assumptions can reflect what we know or, as is often the case, what we think we know. To challenge assumptions:

- State your problem.
- Write down as many existing assumptions about the problem as you can think of.
- Reverse the assumption. Transform it into the opposite of what it is now.
- Modify the assumption. Revise each assumption to make it better or easier to deal with. Change a name, time frame, location, etc. For example, assume that supervisors, rather than department heads, need to approve transactions.
- Vary your perspective. What you see depends on where you stand. Look at your problem from different perspectives.

- Put yourself in different shoes. Try viewing your assumptions from the perspective of another person (your boss, a customer, etc.). Describe the problem from their perspective. Write down new ideas that emerge from looking at things this way.

Solutions Mapping

The objective of this technique is to create better ideas by combining systematic, analytical thinking with spontaneous, unconstrained thinking.

How to Create a Solution Map

- Start with a core premise, validated root cause or the problem statement. Begin brainstorming, forming clusters of related potential solutions around the core premise.
- Using the principles of brainstorming, one person offers an idea and other team members try to expand it, or turn it into another idea.
- Build your solution map as you go so the team can see its ideas begin to take shape.

Five Whys

The objective of this technique is to probe deeper along a particular dimension of thought until you cannot go any further. Probing can go beyond the five levels.

How to use the Five Whys

Start with a team.

- Team asks "Why" the equipment quit working after only 24 hours, and writes the answer below the question that was asked.

- Questions must be asked fewer or more times than five to either find a root cause or a primary solution.

- Team continues asking "Why" the equipment quit working after only 24 hours, until it agrees that the problem's system level root cause has been identified.

- Questions can have multiple reasonable answers. Continue the "Why" question under each possible answer.

- Team determines whether there now appears to be multiple root causes and dependencies. If so, another tool should be used.

There are a number of other techniques available for your use. The key is to adapt ones that align with your organization culture and use them to support your innovation activities.

- Mind-mapping
- Random word
- Idea box
- Twenty questions

- Candid comments
- Musical chairs
- SCAMPER
- Building on ideas

6: CULTURE CHANGE

Establishing the right culture to support innovation and continuous improvement is a necessary prerequisite to achieving success with the OAK principles. A key question that comes up then is: how do you strategize growth within the culture dimension of the organization?

Jeff DeGraff, Dean of Innovation at the University of Michigan describes four types of innovation.

Create type of innovation that pursues radical breaks from the past and develops breakthrough ideas and new things.

Control type of innovation representing those who want controlled incremental change that is systematic and practical. They put a premium on doing things right above all else.

Collaborate type of innovation strives for shared ownership focusing on shared values and communications. They want to do things that last.

Compete type of innovation wants to do things now and appreciate the intensity of competition and achievement.

The phase gated review process takes advantage of these types of innovation culture to maximize speed to market while reducing risk. Create form of innovation is predominant at the beginning of the process as it provide the environment for developing new things in order to compete with larger established organizations. Once a concept is developed, control type of innovation brings a sense of urgency to lead the project. Together with the control and collaborate types of innovation, the complete type takes the idea from concept all the way to prototype.

Members of Research and Development (R&D) teams will typically exhibit cultural characteristics of the create type of innovation. Characteristics of compete type of innovation will be seen in Project Team Leaders. And Project Core Team will bring to the table the collaborative characteristics necessary to engage and establish long term sustaining processes.

In the phase gated review process, collaboration becomes the dominant type of innovation once an idea has attained a definitive prototype status.

At this point it becomes important to incorporate concerns of stakeholders such as customers and shareholders, into something can be sustainable long term. Finally, once the idea has matured and almost ready for prime time, it needs structure to assure consistent delivery – the control type of innovation becomes the dominant form.

Since the phase gated review process is relying on these different types of innovation cultures to be present in order to push an idea from concept to final product, it is imperative that an organization understands how it stacks up in this culture continuum.

As important as it is to have a good strategic roadmap and the knowledge to execute, not having the right organizational culture can compromise those attributes.

Companies that have a history of operational success typically have built the underlying culture over extended periods of time or years. In a sense, when you are a building a new organization from scratch, you have the benefit of a blank slate to define the norms for that organization's culture. You can create and set the tone exactly the way you want to support the vision of the organization.

In contrast, when you are working with an existing organization that has been around a while, norms are already in place so you have the additional challenge of molding or changing the existing into the new.

Question then is how does one realign the culture to support a new vision or direction in other to improve performance? This entails injecting a sense of urgency and energy into the group to get them motivated to buy into the new program and understand the need for change.

So how do you do that? There are multiple ways. In the next few sections I will be describing a five step tried and proven approach that has been used at companies like GE and Johnson and Johnson.

Don't Gamble with Success

Now before I get into it, one can argue that you can take a "preacher sermon" approach whereby you basically preach to the organization and they buy into it—in other words put the fear of God in them to achieve buy-in. This approach is like rolling the dice. It may work or it may not. When you want success you can't afford to gamble. You have to take an approach that will deliver dividends.

So in this approach you're looking at 5 steps. I will first describe the five steps and then go into the details of the steps later on.

- Self-assess and prioritize
- Develop competencies, solutions, and roadmap
- Roles and responsibilities
- Establish rhythm
- Establish operational metrics

The first step is figuring out what the key strengths are of the organization versus the weaknesses in your organization.

The key is to preserve the strengths while addressing the weak attributes. When looking at the weakness of the organization one of the key things you need to understand could be how well your organization is performing against the organization's business objectives.

This results will provide insight on areas of the business where the magnitude and speed of innovation may not be generating the requisite results. The second set of criteria is going to be internal to the team in terms of their feedback on the organization and its culture.

So you develop two sets of criteria. The first one is quantitative and more focused on the results of the team's performance relative to clearly defined business performance goals. The second set is more qualitative and is based on the team's assessment of the organization culture including team dynamics.

Take a Look at Yourself

Generally the first set is relatively easy because you are looking at business goals that are more quantitative and objective. They are either achieved or not and one can easily assess how well. Such measures could be things like revenue, customer wait time, customer growth, supply chain fulfillment, or it could be customer attrition—basically any number of hard metrics. With these metrics you can assess relative to your target and understand how well you are doing relative to your competition as well.

Now with the second set of assessment we are looking at the organization, its structure and team dynamics. This is basically an organization climate survey or employee survey. It is intended to provide an indication of how well the team feels empowered to do the work that they've been charged to do. So in this regard we're trying to assess whether the employees feel engaged or energized to do their work and the reasons behind. Between these two assessments you get a sense for the areas of opportunity that need to be worked on to make progress.

Amortize that Data

Develop solutions and a roadmap. This requires both creativity and a general sense of urgency to accomplish. Recall previously we discussed the need to have clear strategic goals. The assumption here is that we will need to develop solutions to address the gaps that are not supporting our strategic goals. Likewise we need to develop the set of competences and domain expertise required to support the desired culture.

The recipe here is to pull key stakeholders together as a team with a sense of urgency that will feel fully empowered to come up with solutions. This is a good time to get the team and the organization to understand the imperative for change. Any number of improvement tools can be used to prioritize and develop the solutions. Resulting solutions may need to be piloted first before rolling out but regardless, it is important to include key stakeholders in the rollout implementation in order to improve buy-in.

Establish clear identifications of roles and responsibilities. Who is playing what position? The analogy here might be a football team where the quarterback player is on point for throwing a pass to gain yards, and others have responsibility to protect him from a tackle. Everybody playing their position enables the team to execute their plays. This helps in decision-making.

Get the Beat

You must define a rhythm for the organization. Now that everybody understands the role they play we need to make sure we have a mechanism to rally everybody in sync. It's not unlike the boat crew where they sync with each other to the same rhythm in other to maintain the speed and direction desired by the team. Can you image if the crew was rowing without a rhythm? Likewise for an organization and its business process to work well everybody needs to understand the timing for key business events such as accounting closing activities, weekly and or monthly business reviews.

Don't Spare the Yardstick

Operational metrics ties everything together. Recall the organization is on a journey to achieve specific goals. That journey is measured in order to determine how far we have traveled and how much more there is left to go. Having a set of metrics that reflect progress towards your strategic goals is very critical. Progress on these metrics can then be reviewed regularly as part of the organization rhythm. Corrective actions should be assigned to specific owners for resolution.

Conclusion

When we look at the elite club of companies with sales in excess of $1B, it is clear their strategies are as diverse as the products and services they offer their customers. From the hyper-growth new companies such as Amazon.com and the Apple Incs. to the storied names such as Johnson & Johnson and the IBM's whose formation pre-dates the last world war, one finds a common theme in their success: their ability to execute their strategic and operations plan.

Strategic and Operational excellence in essence is foundational for growth. It is about getting an entire organization to execute as if individually it is their company (or they own the success of the company). It is also about continually improving upon customers' perception of value.

The journey achieves and sustains success when everybody aboard is a crew member and not just passenger. That means a roadmap that is devoid of unnecessary complexity, with clear mile markers to track progress.

Key initiatives on the journey have clear specific OAK—an Owner who is Accountable for its success and has access to the Knowledge or tools to complete. It also means clear alignment within the team on the key strategic initiatives that are critical to the journey.

Enrolling the entire organization to adopt the principles of strategic and operational excellence allows an organization to more effectively unleash the creativity and talents of team members, thereby greatly enhancing value delivered to customers and shareholders.